The Dolphin

Prince of the Waves

Text by Renée le Bloas and Jérôme Julienne

READER'S DIGEST
Animal Close-Ups

This edition is published by Reader's Digest Young Families, Inc.
Pleasantville, NY 10570
www.readersdigest.com

Copyright © Éditions Milan 1996. Toulouse, France.
Original edition first published by Éditions Milan under the title *le dauphin, prince des vagues*
French series editor, Valérie Tracqui
Translated by Boston Language Institute

Copyright © 1997 in USA by Charlesbridge Publishing, Watertown, MA.

cover photo "© Bruce Coleman, Inc./Tom Brakefield 1999"

Bottle-nosed dolphins live in all the oceans on our planet, except for those in the polar regions. Some live close to the shore while others live far out at sea.

Strange call!

All is calm in the bay. On the beach, the coconut palms sway gently in the wind. Waves break over the reef with a muffled rumble. The turquoise lagoon shelters thousands of tropical fish that are weaving their way through the coral and anemones.

Suddenly a strange call echoes through the water: "Crreakk, crreakk." It sounds just like a squeaky door. Like a flash of lightning, the streamlined shadow of a torpedo speeds by. It is a dolphin! It leaps out of the water and back down again, shooting up spray.

A few more leaps, then the dolphin swims off beyond the waves. It dives and then disappears.

Nine feet long with 550 pounds of muscle, the dolphin can make unbelievably powerful leaps.

Super swimmer

The dolphin is not a fish. It is a marine mammal, well adapted to aquatic life. It breathes air with its lungs like humans. Its single nostril, the blowhole, is on the top of its head. Because of this, the dolphin can breathe without lifting its whole head out of the water. In the front of the dolphin's head is the rostrum, also called the beak. The beak is a kind of muzzle that the dolphin uses to defend itself. The dolphin has highly developed hearing and a good sense of sight, but it is unable to smell.

The dolphin's well-muscled body is shaped like a torpedo. It can swim, leap, and dive in the waves as it pleases. Unlike a fish's tail, which moves from left to right, the dolphin's powerful tail beats up and down.

With its expressive eyes, the dolphin sees as well in the water as it does in the air.

The dolphin's elastic skin is as soft as velvet. It has almost no hair or pores. The skin is sensitive to the touch, especially around the blowhole.

6

Pointed teeth help the dolphin hold on to slippery prey.

The dolphin blows out a mixture of air and water vapor. Each time it inhales, it replaces ninety percent of the volume of its lungs. Humans only replace fifteen percent of theirs!

So that water doesn't get into the dolphin's lungs, the blowhole closes up with a watertight valve during a dive. Unlike humans, dolphins have to decide to breathe. Because of this, they can sleep for only five or six minutes at a time.

Bottle-nosed dolphins, whose scientific name is *Tursiops truncatus,* usually live in schools of about ten to thirty members. Sometimes they get together to fish in large herds of several hundred dolphins.

The dolphin's flippers act as stabilizers. At top speed, the dolphin can reach about thirty miles per hour.

These super swimmers can dive down more than 1,000 feet in the ocean and stay there for seven or more minutes without breathing.

Thunderbolt of the sea

Behind the coral barrier, two dolphins begin to race. Suddenly one of them bounds across the waves like a skipping stone. It leaps up in the air so it can go even faster, since it is easier to move through air than through water.

Thanks to small sensors in its lower jaw, it is believed that the dolphin can estimate its speed. Its skin creases when it accelerates, absorbing water resistance that could slow it down. The dolphin speeds like a thunderbolt past its companion and finds itself alone in the ocean. Separated from the herd, it is no longer protected from predators. Quickly! It must go back to the other dolphins in the bay.

Dolphins love to swim side by side. Why do they do this? How do they know to make exactly the same movements? This behavior is still a mystery.

A third eye

Darkness falls, and the young dolphin can only see a few yards away. However, thanks to an amazing system of detection called sonar, it has already found its family. Small transmitters located behind its forehead in an organ called the melon send out ultrasounds. These high-pitched squeaks strike the objects around the dolphin and bounce back toward it, like an echo. Even in the dark, the dolphin pictures a three-dimensional image of an object in its brain.

This way of "seeing" is called echolocation. It gives the dolphin a sense of depth and allows it to make out the marine landscape. The dolphin can tell whether an object is lifeless or living, hard or soft. It can also perceive an animal's heartbeats and can tell whether a female is pregnant.

For this dolphin, visiting the murky waters of the mangrove forest is no problem. With its sonar, it avoids the roots of the mangrove trees.

Even in dark, muddy water, the dolphin can detect a penny buried under eight inches of mud!

The dolphin can also get its bearings at night and locate a fish swimming hundreds of yards away. Its echolocation is like a third eye.

This dolphin searches for fish in the sand. It is believed that dolphins stun their prey by sending out ultrasounds.

Although they are bitter enemies, sharks and dolphins sometimes hunt the same school of fish.

In a panic, the sardines draw closer together. Herring, salmon, codfish, shrimp, and squid are also on the hunters' menu.

A fishing party

The dolphins make quite a scene when they go fishing in the bay! A dolphin hunts down a grouper and plays with it like a cat with a mouse. It grabs the fish and then lets it go, only to attack it again.

Suddenly a school of sardines is found at sea. The herd charges, surrounding the fish, forcing them together, and pushing them up to the surface of the water. The dolphins make a lot of noise when they hunt, which helps to confuse their prey. Some dolphins remain farther away from the school of fish. These dolphins capture any sardines that try to escape. The trap is now set. In a swirl of foam, the dolphins take turns and attack their prey. What a feast!

Young love

It is summer and time for the dolphins to mate. In order to simplify courtship, herds of dolphins group together. A competition of acrobatic leaps begins between males over ten years old. They compete with each other for the female dolphins' attention. This mating behavior can last for days.

A couple forms and tries to separate from the others. This is not easy with all the other male dolphins swimming around! Under the turquoise water, the male holds the female between its flippers. Together, they twirl and turn in the water.

After mating, the male and female separate. Each goes off to find another mating partner.

For dolphins, physical contact is essential. It is one of the ways they communicate.

When a dominant male chases a rival, he attacks snout first. Biting and bumping into his opponent, he drives it off with his beak.

While courting, dolphins perform acrobatic feats. They spin around, somersault, and leap almost twenty feet in the air.

A giant baby

Twelve months later, the big day has arrived! The future mother looks for water protected from her enemies. The dolphin has only one baby every three years. When the dolphin calf is born, its "aunt," an older and more experienced female, brings it to the surface. Its blowhole opens, and the baby takes its first breath.

The killer whale, or orca, is an enemy of the dolphin. Hunting in small groups of around fifteen, killer whales may attack as many as a hundred dolphins.

The newborn calf is very large. It is approximately three and a half feet long and weighs about forty-five pounds. In one year, it will be seven times heavier and will have doubled in length.

For four to six years, the young dolphin and its mother are inseparable. Although it also eats fish, the young dolphin continues to nurse for its first eighteen months.

From the time the baby is born, the mother is assisted by an "aunt" dolphin.

The mother lies on her side at the surface. With its tiny beak, the baby dolphin catches hold of its mother's breast. It curls its tongue into the shape of a trough and swallows the concentrated milk that squirts into its mouth.

With its mother's encouragement, the baby tries to swim. Within a half an hour after its birth, it can swim by itself.

These dolphins watch out for the shark that is prowling around the herd.
Many young dolphins are eaten before they grow to adulthood.

At school

Until a dolphin reaches maturity, it attends the school of the deep blue sea. It learns hunting techniques, the languages of sound and sight, the use of sonar, and other survival skills.

Young dolphins are talkative. The bay echoes with many clacking sounds. In order to recognize each other, some dolphins whistle their own theme at the beginning of a phrase. Like humans, each dolphin's voice is unique.

It is playtime! The young friends enjoy wild races and jumping contests. If a young dolphin swims too far away, an adult catches it and slaps it on the back, bringing it back to the herd.

Carried along in their mother's wake, the babies swim easily. They swim close together, fooling their enemies by appearing larger than they are.

A life of freedom

At dusk the sky is purple and gold. Flying fish glide above the water. As it grows up, the young dolphin ventures farther away from its mother. Youngsters remain in groups near the herd until they reach maturity.

When they are about ten years old, the young males will be able to be fathers. The females can have their first baby when they are five to twelve years of age.

Soon the shadow of night covers the vast ocean. Princes of the waves, the dolphins make a last leap in the moonlight and then vanish into the deep. If they avoid sharks, killer whales, fishing nets, and human hunters, they may live to be more than thirty-five years old, free and wild.

Basking in their freedom, dolphins leap in the last rays of the setting sun.

Defenseless dolphins

Although dolphins are protected, loved, and admired by many people, they are still hunted, captured, and drowned in fishing nets by others. Dolphins have little defense against human violence. Even the International Whaling Commission, an organization that regulates the whaling industry, does not protect small sea mammals.

With increased public awareness about the harmful use of nets, changes are beginning to be made. In 1988 the United States banned imported tuna caught by the purse seine nets that kill so many dolphins. In 1992 the United Nations decided to limit the length of drift nets to one and a half miles.

Murderous fishing

Each night all over the world, fishermen drop thousands of miles of drift nets. These long nets are meant to trap fish, but they also catch dolphins by the tens of thousands. The drift nets' danger to dolphins has earned them the title "curtains of death." Another harmful technique is the tuna fishermen's use of purse seine nets. The fishermen use dolphins to locate schools of tuna. Then they surround both the dolphins and the fish with their nets and kill them without distinction. From 1959 to 1972, almost five million dolphins were killed by United States tuna fishermen using purse seine nets.

Dangers at sea

The beaching of sea mammals like the dolphin remains a mystery. Do dolphins lose their sense of direction after big storms? Do parasitic diseases disturb their sense of sonar? Studies of beached animals report illnesses of the lungs, stomach, or blood. The many types of pollution that affect the sea, such as heavy metals, pesticides, and polychlorinated biphenyls (PCBs), are partly responsible for this.

Groups of dolphins that approach humans are rare. At Monkey Mia, part of the local dolphin herd has gotten into the habit of greeting these lucky Australians.

A new approach

Thirty years ago, the behavior of the first dolphins in captivity was fascinating to scientists. At that time, aquariums allowed thousands of people to see unknown species of animals. Today many researchers study dolphins in their natural environment. The study of dolphins in the wild is slowly replacing that of dolphins in captivity.

Dolphins and humans

Dolphins have understood that humans can be useful to them. In Brazil and Mauritania, they work with fishermen by herding the fish into the nets. In Florida, they greet shrimp fishermen as they return from sea. The dolphins are looking for more than friendship, however. Fish in nets or fish thrown overboard are easy meals for these clever dolphins.

Other solitary dolphins sometimes come to meet humans. These dolphins may have been rejected by their herd, or perhaps they are dolphins released from an aquarium. It is not known why these dolphins travel alone, but they most likely seek out humans for companionship.

Aquariums allow us to observe dolphins up close, but it is better for dolphins to remain in their natural habitat.

The Delphinidae

The bottle-nosed dolphin belongs to the Delphinidae family, which contains at least thirty-one species. From the smallest, measuring just under five feet, to the largest, which can reach over thirty feet, many diverse species are represented, including several toothed whales. For all Delphinidae, the first two vertebrae of the neck are fused, limiting their head movement. Some have small beaks, and others have short jaws with large, curved foreheads.

▲

The friendly *pilot whale* usually is found in herds of about fifty members. Sometimes pilot whales live in larger groups of several hundred to more than a thousand members, often joining smaller dolphins and whales. The pilot whale eats mainly squid, and it can dive to depths of more than 2,000 feet.

◀ The *killer whale*, or *orca*, measures just over thirty feet and can weigh up to nine tons. This is one of the largest carnivores on our planet. It does not hesitate to attack large whales and other dolphins. In spite of its reputation, it has never intentionally attacked humans in the wild.

▲
Because they often fight each other, the *Risso dolphins* have skins striped with scars. It is believed that the parallel marks found on many of these dolphins are teeth marks from other Risso dolphins. Other marks may come from fights with squid, whose suckers and claws leave round marks and long scratches.

▲
The *spotted dolphin* lives in tropical waters. Its body is speckled with light spots that appear as it ages. The spots camouflage it from enemies and may also attract fish. They may also be a visual clue allowing the dolphins to recognize each other. Because schools of tuna like to swim with them, the spotted dolphin is most affected by purse seine fishing. Thousands die in fishermen's nets each year.

The *common dolphin* roams the oceans in ▶ giant herds. There are sometimes several thousand of them swimming together. Unlike the bottle-nosed dolphin, the common dolphin refuses to work with humans. It is difficult to train and will let itself die if kept in captivity.

Cetaceans with teeth

Dolphins belong to the toothed suborder of the order Cetacea, called Odontoceti. This suborder includes several other families: sperm whales, narwhal and beluga, river dolphins, beaked whales, and porpoises. The main difference between whales, dolphins, and porpoises is their size, but they have the following in common: a single blowhole, a sense of echolocation, a large skull, and teeth.

▲

The *Amazon River dolphin*, or *boutu*, is very rare. Its beak is long and thin. The boutu's pink skin lightens as it grows older, and it has amazing flexibility in its vertebrae. In the rainy season, it can weave between the trunks and roots of flooded forests. Using sonar, it chases crustaceans and fish in the muddy waters.

◀ The *sperm whale* is found today in all the oceans of the world. The male measures over fifty feet and weighs about forty-five tons. Its enormous head is one-third the length of its body. The female is about forty feet long and weighs about fifteen tons. The sperm whale's body contains a liquid, called spermaceti, that changes density with the temperature. This helps the whale dive as deep as 6,000 or more feet.

The *beluga whale* has a mobile neck. It slices through the vast Arctic waters of Alaska and Siberia. The young beluga is born dark, but the pigments in its skin fade as it grows older. The adult beluga is completely white. Its whiteness may be camouflage that helps it blend in with the ice and escape its predators, the killer whale and the polar bear.

The *harbor porpoise* was once quite common, but its population has been declining in recent years. Still hunted and often a victim of fishermen's nets, it flees from contact with humans. This porpoise was freed from a fishing net. It was tagged before it was released so that scientists will be able to monitor it in its travels. In this way, they will learn more about this threatened species.

For Further Reading . . .

Dolphins (Animal World Series). Donna Bailey. Raintree/Steck Vaughn, 1992.

Friendly Dolphins (Rookie Read-About Science). Allan Fowler. Children's Press, 1997.

Use the Internet to Find Out More . . .

A Directory of Public Aquaria **http://www.actwin.com/fish/public.cgi**
    Find out what aquarium near you has dolphins.

The Dolphin **http://whales.magna.com.au/DISCOVER/DOLPHINS/menud.html**
    Start here for pictures, general information, and a good list of other Web sites.

Dolphins at the Delaware and Ocean City Maryland Beaches
    http://www.beach-net.com/dolphins.html
    This personal site focuses on the Atlantic Bottle-Nosed Dolphin.

The Wild Dolphin Project **http://wwwa.com/dolphin/index.html**

All links were working at the time of publication but may change; we welcome corrections or suggestions for future editions.